THE BATTLE OF PARRAMATTA

—— 21 TO 22 MARCH 1797 ——

T0360113

Jonathan Lim received an Honours degree in Ancient History from Macquarie University in 2002. He practises as a tax lawyer in Sydney. He is a true local of the events of Pemulwuy's war, living in Carlingford on a spot first settled in 1793. He enjoys writing and bushwalking. *The Battle of Parramatta 21 to 22 March 1797* is his first book.

THE BATTLE OF PARRAMATTA

—— 21 TO 22 MARCH 1797 ——

JONATHAN LIM

Australian Scholarly

Persons of Aboriginal or Torres Strait Islander background are
respectfully informed that this book contains references to the dead.

First published 2016 by
Australian Scholarly Publishing Pty Ltd
7 Lt Lothian Street North, North Melbourne, Victoria 3051
tel: 9329 6963 / fax: 9329 5452 / www.scholarly.info

ISBN 978-1-925333-80-0

Cover design by Wayne Saunders

Cover image: Aborigines of a New South Wales tribe forming a spear wall.
Broadhurst Collection of postcards, c.1900–1927, State Library of New South
Wales

Frontispiece: The landing place, Parramatta (c.1809) at foot of High Street. Today
this is the Parramatta Ferry Wharf. The battlefield is to the right. Mitchell
Library, State Library of New South Wales

This book is dedicated, firstly, to my parents and brother, who helped me through the difficult circumstances under which this book was produced; and secondly, to all the surviving members of the Darug Tribe or Nation.

Contents

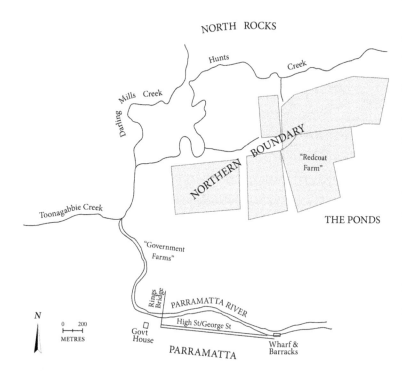

NORTH ROCKS

Hunts Creek

Darling Mills Creek

NORTHERN BOUNDARY

"Redcoat Farm"

Toonagabbie Creek

THE PONDS

"Government Farms"

Rings Bridge

PARRAMATTA RIVER

High St/George St

N

0   200
METRES

Govt House

PARRAMATTA

Wharf & Barracks

Introduction

Where the inhabitants of the quiet Sydney suburbs of Carlingford, Oatlands and North Parramatta now tend their gardens, pick up their children from school and commute sullenly to work on the M54 bus, two contending armies once pursued each other eager for battle. The double pursuit, first by one side, then by the other, culminated in fierce battle in the streets of colonial Parramatta.

My interest in the story of the Battle of Parramatta commenced some years ago when I spent an increasing amount of time walking in the bushland near my home in western Carlingford NSW. I had fond memories of playing in the bushland of the north shore as a child. My sojourns into the bush slowly extended, from half an hour at a time to at least three hours a day. I had time to admire the grey, vanishingly rare turpentine forests, which had once covered large swathes of the Sydney Basin but whose taste for fertile soils made them some of the first bushland to be cleared upon white settlement. I also admired the coachwoods and ferns of the secret pockets of rainforest in the low valleys, and the magnificent prospects of Hunts Creek and Lake Parramatta.

I also increasingly became intrigued by the sandstone caves I found nestled next to the creek. Many of them seemed to have burnt ceilings – a sign of Aboriginal habitation. I even found one cave, which I dubbed 'Six Hands Cave', in which were visible six faded hand-stencils in red ochre – most of the hands apparently being those of Aboriginal children. I then stumbled across rocks bearing the characteristic cigar-shaped grooves of Aboriginal axe-sharpening, as well as trees bearing enormous scars where in former times the industrious ancients had once hacked out water-carriers, bark shields, canoes ...

There is no wonder that I became interested in the early history of my area. I became curious as to when exactly the land on which my house sits was first officially settled. Perhaps it had happened in the 1950s? Perhaps the 1930s? Surely no earlier than that?

The answer, as it turned out, was May 1793. Mr Samuel Barsby, transported for stealing some grey cloth, had settled in the area and had remained, far from his native Exeter, stolidly making a living for nearly thirty years. I then realised that the Battle of Parramatta, which I had vaguely known of since learning about Pemulwuy in school, may have originated in a pursuit of Pemulwuy in the area, conceivably even across Barsby's Farm, in 1797. Such, therefore, is the origin of my interest in the battle.

The Battle of Parramatta is today probably the only reasonably well-known clash between Australian settlers and Aborigines. Pemulwuy himself, mostly on the strength of this battle, has become a major part of the identity of the Aborigines of New South Wales – as witness both the Pemulwuy Project in Redfern and the recently created Sydney suburb of Pemulwuy.

Yet, as will be demonstrated, even scholarly articles, books and museums have scratched only the surface of this fascinating incident. And sometimes they are in what can only be described as total error. I note that the National Museum's rotating exhibit on Pemulwuy in Canberra incorrectly claims that the battle arose because of a raid on farms in Toongabbie; referring to raids by Pemulwuy, to be sure, but the wrong ones and in the wrong area.

Even the more careful authors tend to make the incident seem a mere freak of history, a blundering by one group of people into another followed by brisk, meaningless killing. The truth is far more compelling.

In this book, I will show that there is actually a surprising amount of detail to be gleaned from the original sources about the battle, and the incidents that led up to it. This new detail includes the date of the pursuit and battle, the identity of some of the participants and the location of the battlefield. Some of the consulted sources are obscure and seem never to have been consulted by previous authors on the subject. Other deductions can be made by comparing the primary sources with geography and settlement patterns in early NSW.

Together, they reveal a world that the aforementioned modern inhabitants of Carlingford, North Parramatta and Oatlands would hardly credit; the frontier world of the Northern Boundary settlements, whose early settlers quaked with fear at the horrid presences in the dark wilderness of North Rocks – above all the notorious rebel Pemulwuy and his hostile armies. From the point of view of Aboriginal history, Pemulwuy is revealed to be a true force of history; a master of guerrilla warfare whose path of vengeful destruction did not find its 'last stand' in the Parramatta battle, but actually increased, after his strange death and resurrection, both in intensity and in cunning.

Sources

First, a word about the sources. Authors dealing with the Battle of Parramatta in the past have tended to rely solely on one source, Judge-Advocate David Collins' magisterial *An Account of the English Colony in New South Wales*, which contains a famous one page description of the battle.

However, a second source, not widely available to the public, can tie up a lot of loose ends in Collins' account. This is the somewhat mysterious account by Rev H.W.H. Huntington, his 'History of Parramatta and District' published from 1899 to 1900 in the *The Cumberland Argus and Fruitgrowers' Associate*.

Huntington's newspaper serial, somewhat crudely written but precise in its phrasing, contains an astonishing amount that is not present in Collins, nor in any other source that I can identify.

Grace Karskens uses Huntington, and suggests that he had access to some distorted oral histories from Parramatta, which is just possible.[1] However, I suspect that he instead had access to a (presumably never published) written source, written by a participant in the pursuit and battle. Huntington contains a great deal of circumstantial evidence that cannot possibly have been merely extrapolated from Collins. For example, he dispassionately dates the campaign and battle as occurring on 21 and 22 March 1797. He also includes plausible details, such as Pemulwuy's army taking half an hour to form up and cross the river. As we shall see, Huntington seems to switch to a total reliance on Collins' account only when the shooting actually starts. This makes it seem likely to me that Huntington's source was written by an individual who participated in the pursuit of Pemulwuy, but who fled as soon as the fighting began in Parramatta.

Because Huntington's account is so obscure and may not be available to most people, I have transcribed the entire relevant text in Appendix B to this book.

Two final, even more obscure sources are J.H. Heaton's *Australian Dictionary of Dates and Men of the Time* of 1879 and

John Washington Price's near-contemporaneous *Minerva Journal*. Both seem to include a quantity of relevant material contained in neither of the other sources. These precious scraps I have also transcribed in Appendix B.

Another 'source', as it were, is the geography of the area and the limits of settlement as they were in March 1797. The former can be gleaned by a familiarity with the local landscape and how it shaped life in the area. The latter can easily be deduced from the dates of land grants in the Northern Boundary as of March 1797.

Life on the
Northern Boundary

After the First Fleet landed in Sydney Cove in 1788, Governor Phillip noted that early experiments in agriculture were failing due to the sandy soil of Sydney. For this reason he founded Rose Hill, later Parramatta, upstream amidst more fertile soil.[2] James Ruse demonstrated that farms on the soil around Parramatta were at least theoretically able to sustain themselves. By February 1791 Phillip was desperate to make the colony as a whole able to sustain itself without stored rations. Consequently land grants, including those on the Northern Boundary, were made to convicts who had served their term, on the basis that they would cultivate the grant for a set number of years.

The 'Northern Boundary' got its name from being, as of 1791, the theoretical northern boundary of the Parramatta district settlements. To find it, drive out from Parramatta, travelling north along Church Street and turn right on to Pennant Hills Road. You will now be travelling, from west to east, along the approximate line of the Northern Boundary ridge.[3] Settlement on the Northern Boundary, too, progressed from west to east, as convict settlers sought out the area's welcoming fields of good volcanic soil, along with its fresh air and splendid views.[4]

The settlers of the Northern Boundary were a diverse and colourful lot. For example, the celebrity London pickpocket George Barrington was granted land inside today's King's School. Watkin Tench visited him in December 1791 and was slightly disappointed that the rascally, elegantly-attired, bewigged figure of imagination turned out to be not quite so elegant, and considerably less rascally; he had already been made a constable of Parramatta by that time[5], which caused much amusement back home. Near to Barrington's Farm, John Randall and John Martin received their grants in 1793. They were even odder than Barrington to the modern imagination: black ex-slaves from North America, who escaped their bondage by siding with the

British during the American War of Independence and winning their liberty in return. Those who imagine 'white settlement' might well be surprised at these two gentlemen; John Randall later joined the NSW Corps as a redcoat[6], while Martin married an Irish woman, was singled out by Reverend Marsden as the most hard-working farmer on the Northern Boundary, and later served as chief constable of Parramatta.[7]

Beyond them, on the eastern side of Kingsdene, was settled Samuel Barsby, who bore the distinction of being the first criminal accused (and convicted) in Australian history. He was flogged for assaulting two redcoat marines on the beach at Sydney Cove in 1788.[8] Upon receiving his grant in May 1793 Barsby remained on his land, a hard-working neighbour of John Martin, for nearly thirty years.

By 1797 the Northern Boundary farms extended eastwards from what is now Church Street out to Richard Partridge's enormous farm at approximately what is now James Ruse Agricultural High School.[9] Like most of the early farms in the Sydney Basin, the farms of the Northern Boundary will have mostly been planted with maize-fields, and perhaps peach-orchards; wheat was quite rare.[10] Further, we should not envisage the earliest farms as being neatly cleared patches of land surrounded by bushland. Most farms will have been substantially still populated by native trees, which the freedman farmers often, at most, left as stumps, working around them with hoes, rather than trying the impossible task of dragging them out, or of ploughing the land, without horses or oxen.[11]

We can get a feel for the calendar of life on the Northern Boundary by use of the *New South Wales Pocket Almanack* published in 1806. Maize will have been planted in October each year, with harvest occurring in March and April the following year. Peach trees, meanwhile, were harvested of their fruit gradually from October to December of each year.[12] The distilling of peach brandy was officially frowned upon, but was one of the main attractions of this crop.[13]

By 1797, the dream of the now-absent Phillip seemed to be turning into reality. After several rather ropey years, thanks to hard work, adaptability and toughness, the settlers, including those on the Northern Boundary, were well on the way to turning New South Wales into a thriving colony.

However, watching the tide of settlement were eyes of a very different people, with very different dreams.

Crossing Boundaries

As you travel eastwards along Pennant Hills Road, to your right will be the friendly settled lands of the Ponds, Webb's Farm, and Parramatta itself. But to your left you can still catch glimpses of a much less welcoming country, unsociably hunched and still dark with foliage – the North Rocks, of old sometimes called the Rocks of Jerusalem. You are looking across the frontier of 1797.

Continue eastwards along Pennant Hills Road and turn left on to Bettington Road. There is still a sense of drama, and of crossing boundaries, as you thus descend the north face of the Northern Boundary ridge, down to Hunts Creek and up the other side. Here, the north and east flanks of the Northern Boundary face on to the trackless forests of North Rocks, which concealed a host of dreadful dangers.[14] Even when the observer Watkin Tench inspected the Northern Boundary farms (with evident approval) in December 1791, he reported that attacks by bushrangers and hostile Aborigines already necessitated a corporal and two privates from the NSW Corps being permanently stationed there.[15] By June 1795 five redcoats had actually been granted land in the area (roughly where the Oatlands Golf Course is today), presumably to act as a permanent garrison with even more of a stake in warding off attacks.[16]

Every land grant made to the Northern Boundary farmers was made by the Crown, ostensibly for free. Nevertheless, however blithely the governors may have made their grants, every grant was made at the expense of the Aborigines of the Sydney Basin. The hunter-gatherer practices of the Darug tribe native to the area required an enormous amount of land for each mouth to feed; far more than was required for European agriculture. Even with such a quantity of land, the sparseness and seasonal nature of resources required a constant nomadic movement of the Aborigines through areas they considered to be theirs.

Over time, the Darug will have noticed that the most fertile areas of the Sydney Basin seemed to be increasingly swallowed up by settlement, and to be off limits for their traditional lifestyle. Particularly galling must have been the way the Northern Boundary settlements gradually crept eastwards from North Parramatta. We can imagine the rising tension as one fertile area after another was devoured by convict settlement.

One of those who refused to take this situation was the Darug leader Pemulwuy (c. 1750 to 1802). Pemulwuy appears to be getting more famous every year, as is his war (1790 to 1802), and justly so.[17] He was based apparently in two areas, the area of northwestern Sydney (centred on North Rocks) and an area bordering on to Botany Bay.[18] His guerilla-style attacks, from Prospect Hill in the west to Brickfield Hill in the east, ran rings around what little defensive capabilities were available to early farmers in the Sydney Basin, rarely even encountering prepared resistance. By means of violent raids, Pemulwuy did his best to impede white settlement of the Sydney Basin, causing significant destruction. His warriors murdered whites[19], burned crops[20], slaughtered swine and other animals[21], burned down houses[22] and gathered cobs of maize to sustain themselves in the field.[23]

Death on the Northern Boundary

One of Pemulwuy's favoured targets, and the catalyst for the pursuit and battle of 1797, was the Northern Boundary. The first certain record of a Northern Boundary attack was in late summer (presumably February) 1794, when a skirmish in a maize field resulted in two warriors, probably Pemulwuy's, being shot dead.[24] The maize would have been growing but unripe in February, so we can assume his warriors were not trying to loot, but to burn, the crop – a frequent tactic of Pemulwuy's.[25] This was an occasion when the attackers were apparently surprised and defeated. However, Pemulwuy was rarely detected in his hostile acts; more frequently his forces would be well away before a posse of settlers and soldiers would give pursuit. Such pursuits might result in unreported killings, as many sources hint[26]; some might not. We note that the five redcoats were granted their permanent farm in Oatlands in mid-1795. Possibly the raid of 1794 was succeeded by other Aboriginal raids that made punitive expeditions in response desirable. At any rate, we are informed that it was principally the redcoats rather than the settlers who pressed such expeditions into Aboriginal territory through 1796.

The attacks of 1796

Both Heaton and Huntington state that 1796 was an unusually violent year in the area.[27] An attack on 22 February 1796 seems to have been particularly terrifying and memorable – again note the date, which just precedes the maize harvest.[28] By this time, too, the weird sight of white bushrangers assisting the black warriors in their attacks had become well-known; the increased contempt for firearms shown by Pemulwuy's men was assumed to be due to exposure to such knowledgeable sources.[29]

Huntington implies that punitive redcoat expeditions through 1796 were also severe. Each killing by redcoats may have triggered off a tit for tat mentality justifying Pemulwuy's counterattacks. Through 1796, a further catalyst for revenge attacks appears to be sexual violence directed against Aboriginal women by whites on the Northern Boundary. Huntington seems to imply that such outrages tended to be committed by redcoats who were sent out to pursue Pemulwuy's men.[30]

As the violence intensified through 1796, Governor Hunter issued a greater number of firearms, and recommended that Aborigines be restrained from loitering near the settlements at the Northern Boundary (a policy later imposed more effectively by King). Settlers were also advised to devise a muster system so as to be able to give chase to Pemulwuy's army as soon as the alarm was raised.[31]

The January 1797 Raid

As the maize harvest of March and April began to approach again in 1797, the violence once more increased in intensity. David Collins correctly cites a double murder, of a man and a woman, as the catalyst for the great battle.[32] However, it is only

Huntington who specifies the date of this atrocity as January 1797.[33] The settlers thereupon decided that they must form a posse and chastise Pemulwuy's force (at this point grown to about 100 men) when it next proved possible to find it.

Who was killed on that fateful night in January 1797? Huntington says that the man killed was a 'settler'. (Note that, tellingly, he does not say that of the woman.)[34] If the man *was* a settler, then fortunately enough information survives to suggest that the man must have been one of the redcoats on the Oatlands Golf Club farm. The reason why it must have been a redcoat, is that the other male settlers of the Northern Boundary, as far as one can tell, lived on after 1797 and clearly were not killed then (briefly: Barrington died 1804; Randall 1822; Martin 1837; Barsby 1835; Arndell 1821; Haycock 1798; Parr, Rowe, Carver, Spencer, Partridge, Abrahams and Whiting clearly still active post-1797).

The 'redcoat farm' was granted to four (or perhaps five) redcoat privates of the NSW Corps, whose names were John Abrahams, Joseph Parden, Sam Critchley, James Wherret and John Haycock – the last may have sold out of his grant before the battle, however, and he died in 1798, not 1797.[35] Because Abrahams also lived to post-1797, the victim must have been Parden, Critchley or Wherret. A search of parish records might well turn up the final clue.

At any rate, the woman killed may have been an utterly forgotten common law wife of the deceased redcoat (all the redcoats appear from the size of their respective grants to have been unmarried).[36]

The March 1797 Raid

The settler counterattack in response to this murder did not occur for two months. The final catalyst was the notorious raid of 21 March 1797 (a date we know only from Huntington). Once more, note the coincidence between the ripening of the maize harvest and Pemulwuy's choice of the moment to attack. Now he could cause the maximum damage to the maize crop, as well as feeding his warriors. I also note that the night of 21 March 1797 was moonless – which may have added to the desirability of the date for a raid.[37]

Curiously, like the January attack, the March raid seems to have been directed at the redcoat farm. Both Collins and Huntington declare that Pemulwuy's men ended up with a substantial number of musket-balls and other things looted from 'the soldiers' (only

Huntington identifies these 'other things' as articles of clothing).[38] Some authors have raised eyebrows at the fact that the things were taken from 'soldiers' – this is, of course, explained by the existence of the redcoat farm. If *both* the January and March attacks were directed at the redcoat farm, which seems likely, there is all the more reason to regard them as revenge attacks for killings or sexual violence by these redcoats as they carried out their punitive expeditions through 1796.

We can imagine Pemulwuy taking the soldiers' clothes and musket-balls as a sign of his bravado, and possibly with some idea that the loss of the musket-balls might reduce the redcoats' firepower. At any rate, as well as looting the redcoats' clothing and musket-balls, Pemulwuy's men also took a quantity of maize, which had just been harvested at the time. In those days, maize was harvested, husked, and then stored still on the cob. Pemulwuy's men would have looted the whole cobs of corn. Huntington even specifies that the cobs were cached in netbags when retrieved[39], a form of traditional Aboriginal bag which presumably had been prepared in large numbers before the raid.

With Pemulwuy's army now sighted, settlers and soldiers

gathered themselves together at the redcoat farm, armed themselves for the pursuit with muskets and shotguns, and set out.[40]

Which way did they go? To go south, Pemulwuy would have had to pass through some of the most well-established farms in New South Wales, including the whole Ponds district and the farms of Robert Webb and William Reid. Besides which, it is clear from the descriptions that Pemulwuy's men, after the raid, made their way to an encampment where they were engaged in caching the looted supplies. This makes going northwards into the bush more logical. Huntington also makes clear that the pursuit took place in the 'woods' and ended up in 'North Parramatta'.[41]

It is more likely, therefore, that the pursuit went northward, perhaps over John Martin's or Samuel Barsby's farms (today, the Kingsdene area of Carlingford) and thence to the safety of Hunts Creek. Perhaps the pursuit then proceeded westwards along the creek. Indeed, it is still possible to find caves along the yet-wild Hunts Creek with signs of Aboriginal habitation such as scorched ceilings and hand-stencils. I myself have found several such caves with signs of habitation. We might also note that some of the oldest dated signs of human habitation in the Sydney Basin were found in caves along Darling Mills Creek, to the north of Hunts Creek.[42] Whichever route Pemulwuy took, caves of this sort would have been ideal for the caching of his looted supplies. The quantities of corn taken by Aborigines could be enormous; Pemulwuy's son Tedbury once showed his astonished captors a similar cave in North Rocks which contained *half a ton* of looted corn – presumably to sustain his own army in its fight.[43]

We note that the pursuit could have proceeded along any number of routes through North Rocks, so long as they ultimately ended up in North Parramatta.

Numbers

We are told by the sources that Pemulwuy's army, fleeing through the bush with their corn and other goods, numbered about one hundred.[44] Many of the eyewitnesses of the campaign and battle were soldiers, and well used to judging numbers of people by eye. But how large was the settler army which pursued them?

Assuming that only the male civilian settlers and the redcoats were in this group, we can calculate from the population of the Northern Boundary at March 1797 that the maximum number in the posse[45] was fourteen or fifteen.[46] However, this does not take into account convict servants, garrison-redcoats, squatters[47] or sympathetic neighbours, any of whom may have lent a hand.

A surprising revelation in Huntington is that the posse used Aboriginal trackers to assist them – another reason perhaps why the settlers felt more optimistic this time in catching up to Pemulwuy[48].

An incident in North Rocks

The pursuit through North Rocks will have been strenuous, particularly at night; the terrain in the area, even today, is rugged and broken up. During the pursuit under moonless skies of 21 March 1797, the posse encountered several (apparently unrelated) bands of Aborigines with women and children, whom they left unmolested. It was about dawn, 22 March 1797, that they finally sighted Pemulwuy's 100 warriors and prepared to attack. The place is said by Huntington to be 'in the vicinity of North Parramatta and the Field of Mars' (Field of Mars is the ancient parish name of Carlingford) so it may be at the boundary of the two areas.[49]

Around this time, Pemulwuy's army had halted. Given the amount of looted materials recovered here by the settlers, it may be that Pemulwuy's men had halted at this particular location, possibly a cave, in order to cache their looted corn.

The busy men were apparently oblivious to the fact that they were being tracked. The redcoat and civilian members of the posse sneaked up to the encampment and, in the words of Huntington, prepared 'to give the sable warriors a broadside of musketry'.[50] Thus they lined up, silently poured powder and ball down their gunbarrels, tamped it down, and prepared to give fire.

At that point, the native scouts gave a warning, presumably vocal, to Pemulwuy's men.[51] In an instant, it seems, the one hundred warriors realised their situation, observed (according to Collins) that the posse was armed with muskets, and gave flight.[52] The posse may not have fired, or if it did, they did not have any effect. At any rate we are informed that no Aborigine was harmed at this encounter. We are not told what, if anything, happened to the brave Aboriginal scouts who risked their lives in such an extraordinary way. Perhaps they ran away too.

Apparently it was during this incident, as the Aborigines fled, that the settlers saw white men among Pemulwuy's one hundred warriors, a noteworthy and alarming sight.[53]

The Battle of Parramatta

It was now dawn, which would have been at exactly 6.00 am on 22 March 1797[54]. Pemulwuy's force had escaped a potentially deadly surprise attack. The pursuit did not end there; indeed, nothing daunted, the settlers and redcoats were now apparently able to track Pemulwuy's men more closely. They pursued Pemulwuy through the bush 'to the neighbourhood of North Parramatta'[55] – perhaps near the modern Lake Parramatta. Here they halted, utterly exhausted by the pursuit – not surprisingly. They were also concerned about their small numbers compared with those of the enemy.[56] They therefore decided to check in at the redcoat barracks in Parramatta, both to rest and to obtain reinforcements.

The posse broke off their pursuit and entered the town of

Parramatta, probably via the Rings Bridge which existed at the time. (Lennox Bridge was destroyed by a storm in 1795 and still awaited replacement as at 1797; the other bridges did not yet exist). They would have walked east along High Street (modern George Street) until they reached the old Parramatta Barracks, located approximately in what is now Robin Thomas Reserve, the area of parkland to the east of Harris Street and stretching north almost to the River.[57] A painting from c. 1809 shows the area as a dreary place mostly consisting of the muddy bank of the Parramatta River and a few scattered buildings constituting the barracks. A lonely redcoat stands before his guardbox.[58]

However, even as the posse were reporting at the barracks, the town exploded in an uproar. The people of Parramatta shouted that the blacks were coming.[59] Pemulwuy's men, one hundred strong, had been sighted massing on the other side of the river near some of the farms to the north of Parramatta[60] (perhaps the Government farms – today the Parramatta Eels Stadium and the surrounding area). The warriors were armed with the usual flint-edged spears and ornamented shields, and were observed to be wearing red ochre and white pipeclay simultaneously on their bodies[61], the red ochre indicating that they were preparing for combat.[62] No doubt among them Pemulwuy was to be seen, unmistakable, big, bearded and brawny, with one eye and limping on his lame foot. He was likely wielding the *cannadiul* death-spear edged with brilliant red silcrete which was his trademark. Perhaps his son Tedbury, who seems to have liked wearing a captured jacket[63], was also among the massed ranks, and perhaps also some of the mysterious white bushrangers, though it is noteworthy that Huntington does not mention them after the North Rocks ambush.[64]

It took the Aborigines about half an hour to mass on the left bank of the river. Then they crossed the river, 'in battle array' as Huntington puts it.[65] At the time, the only bridge over the Parramatta River was the predecessor of the modern Rings Bridge. However, the river was quite easily fordable where the Barry Wilde Bridge is today, being extremely shallow and filled with many boulders at that point.[66] It was, at any rate, at one of these two points that Pemulwuy would have crossed the river with his army, in front of the open-mouthed spectators from a town just waking up.

It must have been an astonishing sight. The Battle of Parramatta was not a passive affair for Pemulwuy – quite the reverse. He was actually advancing upon the enemy, in front of many witnesses, daring to enter into the town of Parramatta itself, where the settlers will have felt themselves entirely secure. There is no other scene like it in the history of Aboriginal resistance to white settlement.

Presumably 'battle array', as Huntington calls it, means the hundred warriors crossed the river in column formation. Once across the river the Aborigines changed their formation, according to Huntington advancing 'almost in rows, as if in imitation of a detachment of soldiers'.[67] Grace Karskens takes Huntington's cue and suggests that Pemulwuy's men were merely imitating the practices of the redcoats, perhaps under advisement from his bushranger allies.[68] She then identifies another instance of Aborigines forming ranks at the so-called Battle Mountain incident in 1881. However, before modern communications technology, horizontal ranks were simply the natural way for soldiers to fight; and there are numerous descriptions of Aboriginal warriors forming in ranks in the Sydney area, both before and after the Battle of Parramatta.[69] There was nothing unusual in how Pemulwuy's army advanced.

The Aborigines, in full war paint and heavily armed, would have marched eastward in ranks along High Street (the modern George Street). Before horrified onlookers Pemulwuy's warriors passed what are now the Westpac Building, the Officeworks, and the hideously ugly Civic Arcade before forming up to the west of the Barracks parade ground. The most likely point where the battle occurred is approximately at Robin Thomas Reserve where, today, three roads meet: Harris Street, Macarthur Street and George Street. There they halted.

Two hundred metres before them[70] were ranged the posse of the Northern Boundary, consisting of perhaps four redcoats, eleven other settlers, maybe some convict servants, and possibly some native trackers, extra garrison-redcoats and sympathetic neighbours. However, during the half hour that it took Pemulwuy to cross the river, the posse had also been joined by the soldiers of the Parramatta Barracks, massing on the parade ground in a flurry of drumming and alarm bells, maybe between fifty and seventy strong[71] (it is possible that the garrison was smaller than usual due to detachments being posted to farms for the harvest). We know that the settlers and soldiers were lined up simultaneously, because some of the settlers talked to the commanding officer during the battle. Also, as we shall see, one of the settlers most likely was the one who fired upon Pemulwuy himself.

It is clear that, contrary to the impression given in Collins' account, the two armies were in fact probably fairly even in terms of numbers. It is incredible, given the technological differences, that Pemulwuy still presumed to advance his army openly against such a formidable array. However, as discussed above, Pemulwuy (under bushranger tutelage) may by now have become overly contemptuous of musketry, and he had never tested whether musket-armed soldiers could stand up to an attack by massed spearmen. Besides which, by all accounts, Pemulwuy was by this time in a rage.

Pemulwuy walked to the head of his army and presented his manifesto for fighting, a remarkable record of what the man actually thought, of what motivated him. Because we have testimony of what he said, it is likely that he shouted these words in English. We know McIntire the gamekeeper, whom Pemulwuy speared, had learned the Darug language while associating with him and other Aborigines, and he may have returned the favour[72]; Pemulwuy's son Tedbury's warriors once shouted insults at a settler posse in 'good' English.[73]

Pemulwuy 'harangued the whites about the coercive measures taken by the settlers and soldiers to hunt them down as if they were wild animals'.[74] We have seen that Pemulwuy's pattern of attacks in early 1797 indicated a vengeful animus against the soldiers for their punitive expeditions; his words only confirm it. This statement by Pemulwuy, coming from his own mouth before eyewitnesses, is surely one of the most important pieces of evidence for the motivation for Aboriginal resistance against whites in the earliest days.

During the speech, some of the armed settlers spoke quietly to the officer in command and told him that this was indeed Pemulwuy, who had raided them many times, and that he ought to be seized.[75] The officer told one of the redcoats to advance towards Pemulwuy and arrest him. When the redcoat stepped forward, Pemulwuy, still enraged, shouted that he would spear any man that dared to seize him. This apparently put off the terrified private, for he halted. Now the officer angrily ordered forward four other redcoats, who levelled their muskets and attempted to perform this duty. Pemulwuy cast his red-edged spear at one of these four men, hitting and wounding him.[76]

It is at this point that Huntington's account (or rather his source) abruptly breaks off and he starts relying entirely on David Collins' account instead. From this we can deduce that Huntington's unique source was an eyewitness to the battle, who saw everything up to the first act of violence. He may have been a participant who had pursued Pemulwuy during the previous night but broke and fled when the first musket went off. At any rate, from this point we are mostly relying upon Collins alone.

One of the settlers immediately levelled his shotgun at Pemulwuy and pulled the trigger.[77] (We know it was a settler because Pemulwuy was hit by buckshot from a shotgun, whereas the redcoats would have used Brown Bess muskets. Perhaps the gunman was John Randall, an experienced gamekeeper.)[78] Seven pieces of buckshot ripped into Pemulwuy, striking him in the head and torso. It is only necessary for one blast to have caused the notorious 'seven wounds' of Pemulwuy.

An alternative view of what happened is found in the obscure near-contemporaneous account by John Washington Price, a Canadian who visited Sydney in the summer of 1800. He reports testimony that Pemulwuy was shot at by a 'soldier' and fell wounded; that when the soldier charged forward, Pemulwuy unexpectedly twisted around and flung his spear at the redcoat, killing him on the spot.[79] This aberrant account has the advantage of being very dramatic and close in time to the events described, but may be describing an incident before or after the battle, or may be a distorted account of the battle itself. It contradicts the evidence of both Collins and Huntington that Pemulwuy was hit by buckshot, not a musket-ball, and Huntington's claim that the redcoat Pemulwuy hit was wounded and not killed.

At any rate, Pemulwuy lay wounded in seven places. The other warriors, seeing their great leader fallen, cast their spears in a furious volley. One spear slammed into the arm of a second man, a redcoat or a settler who fell wounded.[80] These two wounded men were the only government casualties in the battle (assuming Price's informant was mistaken). The two lines of men now opened up upon each other in earnest, spears, musket-balls and shot flying through the air. No further soldiers or settlers were hit, however. Perhaps the Aborigines would have been wiser to form up fifty metres from the redcoats rather than two hundred, since the range may have been an issue (the maximum feasible range for a woomera-and-spear being about ninety metres).[81] We can imagine the warriors running up to range before discharging their spears, or perhaps they continued to advance after Pemulwuy was threatened with arrest. At any rate, when the gun smoke cleared, five Aboriginal warriors lay dead, and Pemulwuy lay wounded, bleeding from his seven wounds.[82]

Now, Grace Karskens suggests that Pemulwuy's force may have suffered 50 wounded at the Battle of Parramatta.[83] Some other sources have echoed this claim.[84] This suggestion is incorrect. A closer look at the original source, Heaton, shows clearly that Mr Heaton was referring to two different battles in the relevant passage[85] (see Appendix B). The battle in which Pemulwuy was wounded was our Battle of Parramatta in 1797; the battle 'near Parramatta' in which 50 were 'shot' by redcoats was a later battle on 3 May 1804. (An intriguing statement in itself, since I have never otherwise heard of such a battle, presumably fought by

Pemulwuy's son and successor Tedbury – it may be confused with the incident in Pennant Hills casually mentioned in the *Sydney Gazette* as happening in May *1805*.[86] If there was such a gigantic 'Battle of Pennant Hills' however, I have seen no source describing it.)

Aftermath

As Pemulwuy lay there with his sevenfold wounds, it seemed like he had been decisively defeated. Many must have thought the man himself would die. Yet the Battle of Parramatta turned out to be more the start of Pemulwuy's career than the end of it. By the end of April 1797[87] he was recovered from his wounds, and his first recorded attack after the battle occurred at Lane Cove as early as May 1797.[88] Indeed, in many ways Pemulwuy after the battle was more powerful and more vengeful than he was before it, with the year 1798 being a particularly trying one for the settlers.

The reason for this remarkable turn in fate is well-known. Pemulwuy was taken, gravely wounded and presumed dying, to the Parramatta Hospital (roughly where the NSW Registry of

Births Deaths and Marriages is today)[89] where he was treated by the staff and kept with his leg shackled[90]. Pemulwuy slowly recovered over several days. When his wounds were almost healed, he broke out of the hospital (still with shackle on leg), ran to the bush and rejoined his grieving, doubting disciples.[91] This was probably not the first time Pemulwuy had been shot and recovered[92]; but this would have been a more dramatic and joyous occasion.

The word soon went around: Pemulwuy could not be harmed by the white man's bullets.[93] Pemulwuy's army, already formidable, may have swelled greatly in size after his remarkable return from death; his son Tedbury in later years was supposed to have amassed an army of between three hundred and four hundred men[94], which may indicate the sort of numbers available to Pemulwuy at the height of his power. The rumours about Pemulwuy quickly spread to the terrified settlers; John Washington Price reported the widespread story among settlers that Pemulwuy could not be killed with guns, and that he had been shot so many times there were eight or ten ounces (about three hundred grams) of lead in him.[95]

Another curious thing occurred shortly after the battle; the white bushrangers who had stood out so clearly amongst their fellow combatants were now marked for recapture. On 13 May 1797 Governor Hunter issued a proclamation stating that the white bushrangers John Jeweson, Joseph Saunders, John Wilson (the famous 'Bunboe') and Moses Williams had lately been seen assisting the natives in their attacks, and giving them fourteen days to surrender.[96] It seems probable, given the date, that this referred to the incidents of the Battle of Parramatta.

Pemulwuy's raids after the battle through 1798 may have been the most severe of his career, based on what Collins reports. There were attacks at Lane Cove, Kissing Point[97], Toongabbie[98], and once more at the Northern Boundary where, in a single night in late May 1798 Pemulwuy and his men burned down 'several' farmhouses.[99] The Northern Boundary farmhouses were generally noted by both Tench and Collins as unusually substantial buildings.[100] It is tempting to associate the burning with the farmhouses of the three surviving redcoats on the redcoat farm at that date (Haycock had probably sold out). Perhaps this night of horrors was revenge for the defeat at the Parramatta Barracks;

more likely, Pemulwuy was triumphantly showing that he had not been stymied, that he could do what he pleased to the Northern Boundary farms, and nobody could do a thing to stop it.

Nothing, it seemed, could stop Pemulwuy. He had learned his lesson at the Battle of Parramatta and no longer fought open battles against musket-armed men. Now he stuck to the strategy best suited to him. Every month there were more maize-raids, more killings, more burnings, and there seemed to be no end to it.

Conclusion

As we have seen, the Battle of Parramatta was a dramatic and highly visible event in Australian colonial history. Early Aboriginal resistance to white expansion receives its manifesto in the words delivered by Pemulwuy in the only public forum he ever received. Pemulwuy learned a crucial lesson in the dangers of open battle against a gunpowder army. Finally, Pemulwuy himself was unexpectedly raised to legendary status, paradoxically increasing his popularity and power to a massive degree, even though the battle itself was technically a defeat.

Things have changed. The Northern Boundary is now overlaid with prosaic suburbia. But for a local it is still possible sometimes on a March night on the Northern Boundary to imagine the rows of corn ripening quietly on the dark slopes, and to imagine the still quieter Aboriginal warriors, bundles of paperbark smouldering, preparing to light their firebrands and to cast their rage and vengeance against the intrusive settler-farmers and their redcoat defenders. At their head (Collins said he always was at their head)[101] one-eyed Pemulwuy with his red spear would be leading the way through the dark corn-rows, cunning, wrathful, and seemingly unstoppable.

Appendix A

A chronology of events

9 December 1790	Pemulwuy's War officially commences with spearing of McIntire the gamekeeper
22 February 1791	First official land grants on the Northern Boundary
6 December 1791	Watkin Tench visits the Northern Boundary farms, approves their location, but reports that a permanent garrison of a corporal and two privates are already needed for protection from Aboriginal attack
c. February 1794	First described conflict on Northern Boundary, with two Aborigines shot dead in maize field
25 May and 22 July 1795	'Redcoat farm' (Oatlands Golf Course) officially settled with five redcoats

22 February 1796	Pemulwuy makes major attack on Northern Boundary farms. White bushrangers seen among Pemulwuy's warriors
Remainder of 1796	Gov. Hunter distributes additional firearms and recommends a muster system for the Northern Boundary. Redcoat punitive expeditions against Pemulwuy
January 1797	January 1797 raid on redcoat farm possibly in revenge for redcoat punitive expeditions in 1796; a redcoat and a woman murdered
21 March 1797	March 1797 raid on redcoat farm. Pursuit by redcoats and settlers into bushland of North Rocks
22 March 1797	Failed ambush in bushland north of Parramatta. Pemulwuy pursues redcoats and settlers. Battle of Parramatta. Pemulwuy wounded
c. late March to April 1797	Pemulwuy breaks out of hospital and rejoins army
May 1797	Pemulwuy resumes attacks by this time at the latest
Late May 1798	1798 raid on Northern Boundary, possibly in revenge for Battle of Parramatta

Appendix B

Four sources

The sources on the battle are, other than that of David Collins, difficult to obtain. I have therefore decided to transcribe the full text of all four sources, starting with Collins, to permit the reader to form his or her own judgment on the observations made in this book.

The Collins account

While the governor was endeavouring to guard against the injuries that might be done by these people [i.e. bushrangers], the settlers found themselves obliged to assemble for the purpose of repelling the attacks made upon them by the natives.

The people at the northern farms [i.e. the Northern Boundary] had been repeatedly plundered of their provisions and clothing by a large body of savages, who had also recently killed a man and a woman. Exasperated at such cruel and wanton conduct, they armed themselves, and, after pursuing them a whole night, at sunrise in the morning came up with a party of more than a hundred, who fled immediately on discovering that their pursuers were armed, leaving behind them a quantity of Indian corn [i.e. maize], some musket-balls, and other things of which the soldiers had been plundered.

They continued to follow, and traced them as far as the outskirts of Parramatta. Being fatigued with their march, they entered the town, and in about an hour after were followed by a large body of natives, headed by Pe-mul-wy [*sic*], a riotous and troublesome savage. These were known by the settlers to be the same who had so frequently annoyed them; and they intended, if possible, to seize upon Pe-mul-wy; who, in a great rage, threatened to spear the first man that dared to approach him, and actually did throw a spear at one of the soldiers. The conflict was now begun; a musket was immediately levelled at the principal, which severely wounded him. Many spears were then thrown, and one man was hit in the arm; upon which the superior effect of our fire-arms was immediately shown them, and five were instantly killed.

However unpleasant it was to the governor, that the lives of so many of these people should have been taken, no other course could possibly be pursued; for it was their custom, when they found themselves more numerous and better armed than the white people, to demand with insolence whatever they wanted; and, if refused, to have recourse to murder. This check, it was hoped, would have a good effect; and Pe-mul-wy, who had received seven buck shot in his head and different parts of his body, was taken extremely ill to the hospital. This man was first known in the settlement by the murder of John McIntire in the year 1790; since which he had been a most active enemy to the settlers, plundering them of their property, and endangering their personal safety.

David Collins, An Account of the English Colony in New South Wales, Vol. 2, London, 1802, pp. 19 and 20

The Huntington account

No. XXVIII

[...]

First Black War Scenes in Parramatta in 1796 and 1797

The attacks and depradations to which the settlers in the neighbourhood of Parramatta were exposed during the years 1796 and 1797, from the natives, induced the Governor [i.e. Hunter] to call upon the settlers to afford each other immediate assistance upon occasions of alarm, by assembling when any body of natives were known to be lurking about the farms. Hitherto, mutual assistance, in times of danger, had been more honoured in the breach than in the observance, therefore, the Governor to prevent the frequent murders and robberies by the natives, strictly enjoined the settlers to assemble together for mutual aid, the moment any alarm was given.

On 22nd February, 1796, the natives were very troublesome in our district and at the Hawkesbury. On many occasions escaped convicts were seen amongst the natives, whom they directed and assisted in acts of hostility. Firearms had been given to the settlers and others [i.e. convict servants] for their protection only, but the Governor's positive injunction to them was that they should not wantonly fire at or take the lives of any of the natives as such an act would be considered deliberate murder. The Governor also strictly forbade the settlers encouraging the natives to lurk about their farms, as harbouring them made them troublesome and dangerous.

Notwithstanding every precaution, there was a continual repetition of the most cruel outrages by large bodies of natives throughout the year 1796, on the farmers living on the outstkirts of our town. It was a 'war to the knife' policy between the black and white races. Whenever the military were sent out the chastisement was very effective, but by no means provocative of peaceful results. Many native women were subjected to brutal outrages and the complaining husbands have often been cruelly treated by some of the settlers, while on the other hand the natives plundered the farms of their provisions and clothing, very often wounding their persons and destroying our property.

In January, 1797, one of our settlers and a woman were killed by the natives in our district, which compelled the settlers to arm themselves and make an effort to resent the cruel and wanton outrages of the natives, who frequently deprived them of their livestock, burning their houses and spearing the farm labourers. The exasperated farmers frequently made sorties on the camps of the blacks, where it may reasonably be imagined, a wholesale slaughter was the usual mode for revenge adopted.

On March 21, 1797, the Parramatta farmers formed themselves into a small army and went out into the bush 'man hunting.' During that night they pursued several small parties of blacks with their wives and children, but refrained from wounding or slaying any of them. At last they encountered an army of black warriors numbering over 100 strong, within the vicinity of North Parramatta and the Field of Mars, [*sic*] Just as the settlers were preparing to give the sable warriors a broadside of musketry, some of the native scouts warned their countrymen of the intended onslaught. All of a sudden the natives decamped, leaving behind them some bundles of spears and native weapons, also some nets of stolen corn [i.e. maize], as well as some musket-balls and clothing. It was believed that some runaway convicts were among this tribe of natives, who made off towards Parramatta [i.e. westwards].

[to be continued]

No. XXIX

Sanguinary Battle in the Heart of Our Town in March, 1797

The subjection of the natives to British rule was strikingly demonstrated in March, 1797, by a stand-up fight between the military and a band of natives, resulting in the loss of several lives and many being wounded. The armed settlers (on March 22nd, 1797) were nothing daunted by the retreat of the natives and determined to revenge the recently committed murders [i.e. of January 1797]. They traced the sable warriors to the neighbourhood of North Parramatta. Here the settlers found themselves quite exhausted by their toilsome march through the woods on the previous day and night.

After a conference they resolved to enter our town [i.e. Parramatta] and seek for military assistance as the blacks were preparing for a battle royal. They had hardly entered the town and made known the object of their errand at the barracks, when there was a great commotion and consternation in our streets among the householders, who were running about crying out, 'Help! help! the blacks are coming.' This piece of intelligence had been communicated to them by settlers just arrived from the neighbouring farms, where they had witnessed the mustering of the blacks near their homes.

Without delay the drums beat to arms, and the alarm bell rung [*sic*]. Within half an hour of the arrival of the armed settlers the military and others, fully armed and accoutered, assembled on the parade ground. At the same time upwards of 100 natives armed with shields and spears and their faces and bodies painted with streaks of red and white clay were to be seen marching in battle array across the river. The native chieftain, Pemulwy [*sic*], headed the sable warriors, who marched almost in rows as if in imitation of a detachment of soldiers.

They haltered [*sic*] within a couple hundred yards of the drawn-up white military forces. Pemulwy then harangued the whites, on the coercive measures taken by the settlers and soldiers to hunt them down as if they were wild animals [...]

[A description of Pemulwuy's career, based apparently on Collins, is here excised.]

[...] While Pemulwy was addressing the military on the native grievances, the armed settlers told the officer in charge that Pemulwy was a riotous and troublesome savage, also that he and his tribe had frequently annoyed them, and further they intended, if possible, to seize him. A soldier was thereupon told off to approach Pemulwy, who in a great rage threatened to spear the first man who dared to place a hand on him. Four other soldiers were then ordered to advance and seize him, whereupon Pemulwy threw his spear and wounded the foremost soldier [...]

[As discussed above, the account then follows Collins entirely.]

H.W.H. Huntington, 'History of Parramatta and district,' in The Cumberland Argus and Fruitgrowers' Advocate, 1899–1900, Nos XXVIII and XXIX

The Heaton account

ABORIGINALS

[...]

[...] ***ATTACKS BY.*** Very troublesome in 1796; people at farms about Parramatta plundered of provisions and clothing; settlers armed themselves, and several conflicts ensued throughout the year; many blacks were killed and several of the Europeans were wounded [...]

[...] ***CONFLICTS WITH.*** Near Sydney, August, 1794; desperate fight at Parramatta (their leader Pemulwy [*sic*] wounded and captured), March, 1797; near Parramatta (between natives and military – 50 natives shot), May 3, 1804; [...]

J.H. Heaton, Australian Dictionary of Dates and Men of the Time, Part II, London, 1879, pp. 2–3

The Price account

Among these chiefs [of Aboriginal tribes or families], some of them are exceeding [*sic*] brave and courageous, [*sic*] there is now one called Pummil-woy [*sic*] (who frequents Sidney [*sic*] and Paramatta [*sic*]) & who having killed some of our people an order was given to shoot him, yet few that have attempted it but he has speared, [*sic*] not long since a soldier at Paramatta fired at him, he fell, but before the soldier charged again he turned round, threw his spear and killed him on the spot; he has since recovered and has been known to say 'that no gun or pistol can kill him', many shots have been fired at him and he has now lodged in him, in shot, sluggs [*sic*] and bullets about eight or ten ounces of lead, it is supposed he has killed over 30 of our people, but it is doubtful on which side the provocation was given.

John Washington Price, The Minerva Journal of John Washington Price, Melbourne, 2000

Bibliography

Val Attenbrow, *Sydney's Aboriginal Past*, Sydney, 2002

Terry Cass, Carol Liston and John McClymont, *Parramatta: A Past Revealed*, Parramatta, 1996

David Collins, *An Account of the English Colony in New South Wales*, 2 vols, Sydney, 1975

John Connor, *The Australian Frontier Wars*, Sydney, 2002

Al Grassby and Marji Hill, *Six Australian Battlefields*, North Ryde, 1988

J.H. Heaton, *Australian Dictionary of Dates and Men of the Time*, facs ed., New York, 2011

Historical Records of Australia, Sydney, 1914

Historical Records of New South Wales, Sydney, 1892

John Hunter, *The First Fleet Journal*, Malvern, 2011

H.W.H. Huntington, 'History of Parramatta and District', in *The Cumberland Argus and Fruitgrowers' Advocate*, 1899–1900, nos XXVIII and XXIX

Grace Karskens, *The Colony: A History of Early Sydney*, Crows Nest, 2009

Doug Kohlhoff, 'Did Henry Hacking shoot Pemulwuy? A reappraisal', in *Journal of the Royal Australian Historical Society*, vol. 99, part 1, June 2013

John McPhee (ed.), *Joseph Lycett, Convict Artist*, Sydney, 2006

John Washington Price, *The Minerva Journal of John Washington Price*, Melbourne, 2000

Cassandra Pybus, *Black Founders*, Sydney, 2006

R.J. Ryan (ed.), *Land Grants*, Five Dock, 1974

Watkin Tench, *1788*, Melbourne, 2009

Pam Trimmer, *Carlingford Then and Now*, Sydney, 2006

Notes

HRA Historical Records of Australia
HRNSW Historical Records of New South Wales
NSWSC New South Wales Supreme Court

1 Karskens, p. 477.

2 Ibid., p. 107.

3 Some authors like Grassby and Hill (a problematic source) seem to
   identify the Northern Boundary with Toongabbie, for some reason
   (p. 98); Karskens, p. 111, identifies it with North Rocks – the reality
   is clear once careful comparison is made of the parish maps.

4 Tench, p. 218; Karskens, p. 112, albeit discussing the Dundas Valley
   slightly to the south; Phillip to Dundas 19 March 1792, from
   HRNSW, vol. 1, p. 599.

5 Tench, p. 244–5.

6 Pybus, pp. 141–2.

7 Ibid., pp. 155–6; Hunter to Portland, 2 March 1798, *HRA*, vol. 2,
   p. 142.

8 Ryan, pp. 12 and 15; *R. v. Barsby* [1788], NSWSC 1.

9 Ryan, p. 68.

10 Hunter to Portland, 20 August 1796, *HRA*, vol. 1, p. 596.

11 Karskens, pp. 112–14.

12 *New South Wales Pocket Almanack and Colonial Remembrancer 1806*, pp. 15–17, 22–25; although note that according to Karskens, p. 116, the ideal in the *Almanack* did not always reflect reality on the farms.

13 Karskens, pp. 268–9.

14 Ibid., p. 298.

15 Tench, pp. 216–18.

16 Ryan, p. 50.

17 Kolhoff, p. 77.

18 The areas claimed by the Bidjigal Clan of the Darug Nation have caused some controversy, with some arguing that the word 'Bidjigal/ Bediagal' referred to a kind of priestly caste within each clan. This ignores the fact that Pemulwuy was plainly active in the Botany Bay area when he was pursued by Watkin Tench's campaign of 1790, so his having two areas of operation is at least supported by his physical presence. I would suggest that the solution to the problem may lie in the fact that Sydney area Aborigines frequently intermarried between clans, which would give each family two 'homelands' as it were. See Attenbrow, pp. 58–60.

19 Collins, vol. 2, p. 20.

20 King's proclamation of 22 November 1801, *HRA*, vol. 3, p. 466.

21 Collins, vol. 2, p. 25.

22 Ibid., pp. 25, 83.

23 Collins, vol. 1, p. 348, albeit again discussing the possibly unrelated Hawkesbury war; Grassby and Hill purport (p. 98) to set forth Pemulwuy's wider strategy, to attack Toongabbie farms in order to split off communication between the Hawkesbury and Parramatta, and then to attack Parramatta itself. There appears to be no evidence

for this idea; quite apart from the fact that the Northern Boundary is to the *east* of Parramatta and not to its west.

24 Pybus, p. 132.

25 King's proclamation of 22 November 1801, *HRA*, vol. 3, p. 466.

26 Huntington, No. XXVIII; Karskens p. 465.

27 Heaton, part II, p. 2; Huntington, No. XXVIII.

28 Huntington, No. XXVIII.

29 Hunter to Portland, *HRA*, vol. 1, p. 554.

30 Huntington, No. XXVIII.

31 Ibid.

32 Collins, vol. 2, p. 20.

33 Huntington, No. XXVIII.

34 Ibid.

35 Trimmer, p. 68.

36 Ryan, p. xiii.

37 Nasa's moon chart website, http://eclipse.gsfc.nasa.gov/phase/phases1701.html.

38 Collins, vol. 2, p. 20; Huntington, No. XXVIII.

39 Huntington, No. XXVIII.

40 Again, Grassby and Hill at p. 98 identify the pursuers as being from the Toongabbie farms for some reason; in addition, they make the odd claim that the settlers were mounted, for which there is no evidence.

41 Huntington, No. XXIX.

42 Attenbrow, p. 20.

43 *Sydney Gazette*, 19 May 1805, pp. 2–3.

44 Collins, vol. 2, p. 20; Huntington, No. XXVIII.

45 I have used the inadequate word 'posse' to describe this band of avengers; 'whites' is no good since two of them may have been black, not to mention the Aboriginal trackers; 'settlers' would leave out the soldiers and vice versa, and 'militia' implies some sort of official status.

46 John Rowe, Joseph Carver, William Parr, William Whiting, Thomas Arndell, George Barrington, John Randall, John Martin, Samuel Barsby, Daniel Spencer, John Abrahams, James Wherret, Joseph Parden, Sam Critchley (albeit minus one of the preceding three who was killed), John Haycock (possibly), Richard Patridge.

47 Simon Burn had been tragically murdered in 1794 and his abandoned farm may have been occupied by a squatter.

48 Huntington, No. XXVIII.

49 Ibid.

50 Ibid.

51 Ibid.

52 Collins, vol. 2, p. 20.

53 Huntington, no XXVIII. Note that Grassby and Hill (p. 98) claim that Pemulwuy's attack on the Northern Boundary was a successful attempt to split off Parramatta from the Hawkesbury (which is geographically impossible), that the settlers actually covered up the extent of their 'defeat' at their farms, and that Pemulwuy made multiple guerrilla attacks on the settlers during the night-pursuit. They claim that the true state of affairs is revealed by the fact that the posse was 'fatigued' the next day. All these claims appear to be without basis in any source.

54 Collins, vol. 2, p. 20; Time and Date website http://www.timeand-

date.com/worldclock/astronomy.html.

55 Huntington, No. XXIX.

56 Collins, vol. 2, p. 20; Huntington, No. XXIX.

57 Kass, pp. 24–5.

58 Kass, plate 4.

59 Huntington, No. XXIX.

60 Ibid.

61 Ibid.

62 Price, p. 173; McPhee, p. 106.

63 *Sydney Gazette*, 19 May 1805, p. 3.

64 Huntington, No. XXIX.

65 Ibid.

66 Kass, plate 5 caption. This may possibly, by the way, be the origin of the word 'boromeda/parramatta', since the eels would be obliged to slide on their bellies upstream when going up to breed – Huntington mentions a theory of the sort.

67 Huntington, No. XXIX.

68 Karskens, pp. 476–7.

69 Eg. Hunter, p. 30; *Sydney Gazette*, 2 September 1804, p. 2; illustrated in Lycett's painting of an Aboriginal attack on a boat, McPhee, p. 116.

70 Huntington, No. XXIX.

71 Collins, vol. 1, p. 168.

72 Tench, p. 165.

73 *Sydney Gazette*, 9 June 1805; Karskens, p. 484.

74 Collins, vol. 2, p. 20; Huntington, No. XXIX.

75 Huntington, No. XXIX; note that Collins, vol. 2, p. 20 mentions the men being 'determined' to seize Pemulwuy but does not explain how the attempt was made.

76 Huntington, No. XXIX; this explains the reference in Collins, vol. 2, p. 20 of Pemulwuy threatening to spear the 'first' man who dared to approach him – i.e. the first of the five men who eventually approached him. Note that Collins does not say whether the first redcoat casualty was killed – only Huntington makes clear that the man was wounded.

77 Collins, vol. 2, p. 20.

78 Pybus, p. 129.

79 Price, p. 174.

80 Collins, vol. 2, p. 20.

81 Hunter, p. 56, footnote. Grassby and Hill, p. 99 state that the two forces were 90 metres apart, but cite no source.

82 Collins, vol. 2, p. 20.

83 Karskens, p. 476; followed for example by Dictionary of Sydney website http://dictionaryofsydney.org/entry/pemulwuy.

84 The claim may originate from Grassby and Hill, p. 99.

85 Heaton, part II, p. 3.

86 *Sydney Gazette*, 19 May 1805, p. 2.

87 Collins, vol. 2, p. 24.

88 Ibid., p. 25.

89 Kass, p. 25.

90 Collins, vol. 2, p. 20.

91 Huntington, No. XXIX.

92 Price, p. 174; Collins, vol. 1, p. 371, although perhaps Black Caesar did not shoot him.

93 Collins, vol. 2, p. 70; Price, p. 174.

94 Karskens, p. 484.

95 Price, p. 174.

96 King, General Order 13 May 1797, from *HRNSW*, vol. 3, pp. 208–9.

97 Collins, vol. 2, p. 25.

98 Ibid., p. 66.

99 Ibid., p. 83.

100 Tench, p. 218; Collins, vol. 2, p. 83.

101 Collins, vol. 2, p. 70.

9 781925 333800